AMAZING ANIMALS

Question & Answer Book

by
Judy Braus, Jody Marshall,
Joyce Altman, and Nancy Hitchner

Consultant:
Dr. Michael H. Robinson,
Zoo Director and Tropical Biologist,
Washington, D.C.

TORMONT

Published in 1993 by Tormont Publications Inc.,
338 Saint-Antoine St. East, Montreal, Canada H2Y 1A3
Tel.: (514) 954-1441   Fax: (514) 954-1443
Designed and produced by Joshua Morris Publishing, Inc.,
221 Danbury Road, Wilton, CT 06897

ISBN 2-89429-381-X
Printed in the United States of America
10 9 8 7 6 5 4 3 2 1

Photo Credits: Front and back cover background—Heather Angel/Brian Rogers-Biofotos; p. 56—Miriam Austerman/Animals Animals; p. 91—Michael Dick/Animals Animals. All other photos Bruce Coleman Limited, Unit 16, Chiltern Business Village, Arundel Road, Uxbridge, Middlesex UB8 2SN, England, UK: Front cover, p. 72—Erwin and Peggy Bauer; front cover, pp. 34, 74 (inset), 90, 127—Dieter and Mary Plage; endpapers (front and back), pp. 22, 33, 44, 48, 62 (inset), 84, 136—Kim Taylor; pp. 1, 12, 14, 14 (inset), 17, 46, 60, 69, 82, 89, 95, 106, 116, 126, 133 (inset), 135 (top inset), 140—Jane Burton; pp. 5 (inset), 9—Udo Hirsch; pp. 5 (background), 87, 101 (background), 102, 109 (inset)—Dr. Eckart Pott; pp. 6, 23, 62—John Visser; pp. 7, 26, 64, 107, 125 (background), 129—Hans Reinhard; pp. 8, 80—Christian Zuber; pp. 10, 35 (inset), 37—Dr. M.P. Kahl; pp. 11, 43, 79—Alain Compost; pp. 13, 13 (inset), 21, 122—Leonard Lee Rue; pp. 15, 113—Ken Balcomb; p. 16—Dr. Sandro Prato; p. 18—R.I.M. Campbell; pp. 19 (inset), 31—Sophy and Michael Day; pp. 19 (background), 35 (background), 71 (background), 93 (background)—Mr. Jules Cowan; p. 20—Flip de Nooyer/Havelte-Holland; pp. 24, 55, 58, 68, 71 (inset), 75, 142—Gunter Ziesler; pp. 25, 51—Peter Davey; p. 27—Wayne Lankinen; pp. 28, 39, 104 (inset)—Francisco J. Erize; pp. 29, 47 (background), 81 (background), 119—John Shaw; pp. 30, 41, 103, 135, 138, 138 (bottom inset)—Jen and Des Bartlett; pp. 32, 115, 121—Jeff Foott Productions; p. 36—A.J. Deane; pp. 38, 66—Andy Purcell; pp. 40, 110—Dr. John Mackinnon; p. 42—Allan Power; pp. 45, 83, 120—Konrad Wothe; pp. 47 (inset), 57—Carol Hughes; pp. 49, 67—M.P.L. Fogden; p. 50—Orion Service and Trading Company, Inc.; pp. 52, 97—Mr. Johnny Johnson; p. 53—WWF/Al Giddings; pp. 54, 87 (inset)—Rod Williams; pp. 59 (inset), 70—Giorgio Gualco; p. 59 (background)—Steve Alden; pp. 61, 73 (inset), 101 (inset), 104—John Cancalosi; pp. 63, 139, 139 (inset)—Bob and Clara Calhoun; pp. 65, 98, 125 (inset), 128—Carl Roessler; pp. 74, 94, back cover—Luiz Claudio Marigo; p. 76—H. Rivarola; p. 77—Frans Lanting; p. 78—Mrs. Waina Cheng Ward; pp. 78 (inset), 132—Peter Ward; pp. 81 (inset), 92, 100—Fritz Prenzel; pp. 85, 130—William S. Paton; pp. 86, 73—Michael Fogden; pp. 88, 108 (inset)—Bruce Coleman Ltd.; pp. 93 (inset), 96, 99—Michael Freeman; p. 98 (inset)—Norman Tomalin; p. 105—C.B. and D.W. Frith; p. 106 (inset)—Mark N. Boulton; p. 108—Kevin Rushby; pp. 109, 138 (top inset)—Stephen J. Krasemann; pp. 111 (inset), 114—Frithfoto; p. 111 (background)—Gerald Cubitt; pp. 112, 123—Steven C. Kaufman; p. 117—Robert Glover; p. 118—Peter Davey/ARPS; p. 124—Fred Bruemmer; p. 131—Jon Kenfield; p. 133 (background)—Dr. Scott Nielsen; p. 134—Mr. P. Clement; p. 135 (bottom inset)—Peter F.R. Jackson; p. 136 (inset)—Dr. Frieder Sauer; p. 137—C.C. Lockwood; p. 141—John Markham.

Contents

"In wildness is the preservation of the world."
— Henry David Thoreau, *Walking*, 1862.

All in the Family

Is this crocodile eating its own baby?

No. In fact, crocodiles provide the most parental care of any reptiles and would *never* hurt their young. After a female breeds, she digs a pit and lays from twenty-five to seventy-five eggs in it. She covers the nest with sand and plant matter to keep the eggs warm, and she guards the eggs for three months. When they are ready to hatch, the young use a special egg tooth to break out of the shell. They call to their mother, and she uncovers them, gently carrying them in her mouth to a safe place (as the African Nile crocodile in this photograph is doing). She continues to care for them for another three to six months, as the babies first eat insects and later fish and birds.

Can a kangaroo baby climb out of its mother's pouch?

Yes, but not right away. After a gestation (time spent by a baby inside its mother's body) of just one month, a mother red kangaroo gives birth to one tiny newborn weighing less than an ounce (about twenty-eight grams). The baby, though blind, deaf, and hairless, miraculously finds its way to the mother's pouch. The baby stays there for eight months while the mother hops about the grassy plains of Australia. After that, the baby ventures out but stays close by the mother for another few months. During this period, the baby will climb into the pouch regularly, especially if it's frightened. It goes in headfirst, and then turns around and sticks its head back out.

Why is this baby elephant trying to climb on top of another?

The baby elephant, or calf, trying to climb on top of the other, larger baby is just having some frisky fun. Asian elephants live in herds of mothers and their young, and often two females will give birth at the same time. When this happens, they help care for each other's calves. Since adult elephants spend a great deal of the day eating, one mother will keep an eye on the youngsters while the other eats. Beginning at the age of four, older brothers and sisters also help look after young calves. They will feed them, play with them, and make sure they don't wander away from the herd. In doing so, these older brother and sister elephants are learning how to become good parents themselves one day.

Does a baby tortoise travel on its mother's back?

No. In fact, since baby tortoises are able to take care of themselves and find food on their own right after birth, they don't need to stay with their mothers at all.

Once they have mated, adult female Galápagos tortoises find a spot of bare soil where they dig up a foot-wide (thirty-centimeter-wide) pit. They deposit fifteen to twenty eggs in the pit and then carefully cover it with soil. The young will eventually hatch, dig themselves out, and begin the quest for survival on their own.

This photo shows the difference in size between a tiny 8-day-old Galápagos tortoise and its 150-year-old mother, which may weigh as much as 500 pounds (227 kilograms).

The tortoises are named after the Pacific islands where they live, called the Galápagos, lying west of South America.

Why are these warthogs running?

This small group of warthogs is rushing away from danger. Even though they are armed with pointy tusks, warthogs can't easily defend themselves against some of their larger enemies. So when a predator such as a lion or leopard approaches on the African plains, warthogs will flee at speeds of up to thirty-three miles (fifty-three kilometers) per hour. As they dash off, the warthogs raise their tuft-ended tails and wave them like flags. This "hightailing" serves to warn the other family members to run. For further safety, several groups of warthogs will often band together to form a clan.

Can baby orangutans climb trees?

Not when they're very young. For their first year of life, baby orangutans cling to their mother's fur and seldom leave her side. So as the mother climbs the trees in their South American rain forest home, the babies are always with her. Babies aren't completely weaned (no longer drinking their mother's milk) until they are three years old, but they start eating bits of fruit at four months. Orangutans live alone, with the exception of mothers who are raising their young. Mother orangutans care for their youngsters until they are seven to ten years old and are ready to live on their own.

Why are these little fish coming out of the big fish's mouth?

The African, or Nile, mouthbrooder actually carries its developing eggs in its mouth. This is helpful in two ways: It keeps the unborn fish safe from predators, and it also helps to keep them aerated (supplied with air). The female keeps the eggs protected until they're ready to hatch. This is called *incubation*. When the eggs begin to hatch, the female opens her mouth and lets them out. If there's any danger, the freshly hatched babies will return to their mother's mouth for safety. Mouthbrooders reach a length of twenty inches (fifty-one centimeters) and feed mostly on microscopic organisms (living animals or plants that can only be seen under a microscope).

Do polar bears make good mothers?

The look on the mother polar bear's face (see small photo) as she cuddles with her cubs says it all—polar bears make *very* good mothers. Females usually give birth to one or two cubs and care for them for two and a half years. The females give birth in dens to tiny cubs weighing only a few pounds. Within a few months, the cubs grow considerably and can fend for themselves. They learn how to find food by tagging along with their mother (see large photo) as she locates berries and other available plants they can eat. Cubs also watch and learn from their mother when she hunts for seals, walruses, and fish—the food these Arctic animals like most of all. This preference for meat makes polar bears the largest meat eaters living on land.

Are these three babies home alone?

Just temporarily. The three European wild baby rabbits seen at left are snuggled down in a downy nest made by mother, unseen but getting ready to feed them. When not feeding or tending to her babies, the mother will cover up the nest to keep the babies warm and to hide them from predators.

When a female rabbit is ready to give birth, she digs a shallow hole for a nest, or brood chamber, like this one. She lines the nest with dry grass and soft material. Sometimes a mother rabbit will use her teeth to pluck fur off her chest and line the nest with that. Every night for three weeks, she comes to the nest to feed her young. After that, they can take care of themselves.

Mothers can have up to four litters a year. The baby rabbits in each litter are called kits or kittens.

In regions of cold weather, or during winter, some rabbits (like the one you see at bottom left) live in large burrows under the ground. A whole system of burrows shared by groups of rabbits is called a warren.

How old is this baby whale?

This killer whale baby, called a calf, is only three days old and is busy drinking its mother's milk. Though they live underwater like fish, whales are really mammals. This means that, like all mammals, they are born live (rather than hatched) and are fed mother's milk for the early months or years of life. Killer whales are in the dolphin family, and they live in extended family groups that travel and hunt together for food in cool seas. They eat anything from seals and porpoises to fish and penguins.

What is this orange worm doing in this white, fuzzy case?

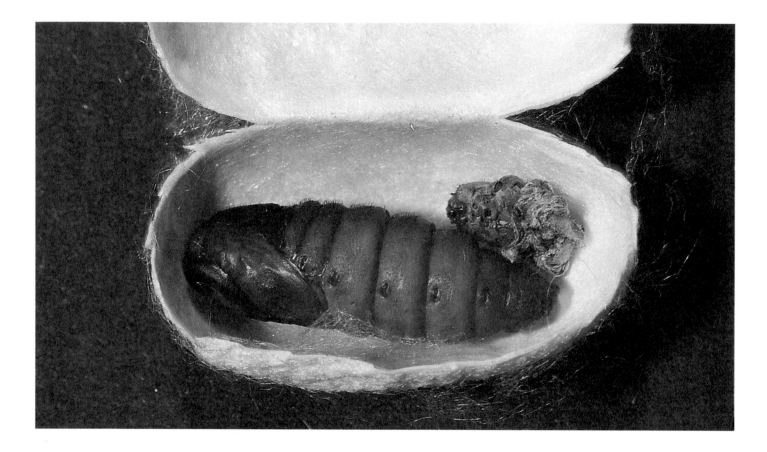

The white "case" is really a cocoon about 1½ inches (3½ centimeters) long. The orange worm resting inside it is the pupa, or immature form, of a mulberry silk moth that has just molted, or shed its shell. (You can see a small heap of molted shell to the right of it.) The silk moth begins life as an egg enclosed in a capsule. It then transforms into a larva (or caterpillar) with a hard shell. Molting, or shedding, occurs whenever the caterpillar's shell is too small to allow for growth. Once it is fully grown, the caterpillar molts for the last time, forms a cocoon of silk, and transforms into a pupa, or chrysalis (the stage between larva and adult). After about a month, the adult moth emerges from the cocoon.

What are the bubbles under this long, tubelike fish?

They're not bubbles—they're actually eggs. In the greater pipefish (sometimes called worm fish) species, it is the male that incubates (keeps protected until hatching) the eggs, not the female. The female lays the eggs in a groove along the male's belly—a double fold of skin that forms a protective pouch—and he carries them until they hatch. After the eggs incubate for five weeks, the young fish come out through a slit where the folds of the pouch meet. Greater pipefish feed on crustaceans (spineless animals like shrimp and crabs), microscopic plants and animals, and small fish in the waters along Europe's coast. The long, thin bodies of the greater pipefish help them to stay camouflaged, or hidden, among the seaweed.

What does a gorilla do in its nest?

Mostly sleep. Every night when the sun starts to go down, mountain gorillas in Africa look for a good spot to spend the night and build what's called a sleeping nest, as seen here.

Gorillas live in family groups called troops. The youngsters sleep in the tops or forks of trees (often with their mothers), while the mature animals sometimes sleep on the ground. Nests are made of shrubs and branches that are bent to form a strong but springy platform.

How would you like to make your own bed each night—actually *make* it from scratch? Well, that's what every gorilla must do, since no gorilla will sleep in the same nest twice.

What's for Dinner?

Did this bird catch all these fish at once?

Yes. This odd-looking bird is the puffin. It lives in the Arctic areas of the Atlantic and Pacific oceans, and its high, flattened bill is perfect for snaring and holding on to more than one fish at a time. Puffins are terrific swimmers and divers, using their wings as paddles and their feet as a rudder. And their white underbellies help hide them from fish below, making it easier to catch them.

Why are this chipmunk's cheeks so fat?

Your cheeks would be fat, too, if you carried your "groceries" home in them. A stretchable skin pouch inside each cheek allows chipmunks to do just that. These little rodents can carry a lot of seeds, acorns, and other food in their cheek pouches. When a chipmunk's cheeks are stuffed to the brim, each one can be nearly as big as the animal's head! Chipmunks store their food in their burrows and also under rocks and logs. That way, if they get hungry, they always have a ready supply of snacks—as long as they remember where they've stored their stash!

How fast can this lizard snap out its tongue for a meal?

This Jackson chameleon can shoot its tongue out, zap an insect with the sticky tip, snap the tongue back, and swallow the insect in a single gulp—*all in less than a second!* The whole thing happens so fast that it's almost a blur to the human eye. What's even more amazing is that this five-inch (thirteen-centimeter) tongue is as long as the chameleon itself. When not in use, the tongue is balled up under a special flap inside the chameleon's mouth, ready to spring out again at another victim. And insects aren't the only victims these lightning-tongued African lizards can zap. Some can reel in small mice, other lizards, and even small birds with their sticky tongues.

How can this snake swallow an egg that's bigger than its mouth?

The upper and lower jaws of this African egg-eating snake are loosely joined. The snake also has stretchy tissue connecting the bones in its jaws. These special features allow the snake to open its jaws wide enough to swallow an egg that is bigger than its own head. As muscular action pushes the egg down the throat, the snake's ribs spread and scales stretch to make room. But swallowing something this big takes time—often more than half an hour.

How can this bird stay still in the air long enough to feed?

By beating its wings at a fantastically fast rate! Like all hummingbirds, Chile's greenback fire-crown hummingbird can beat its wings between fifty and seventy times per second. That's just a blur to the human eye. The rapid wing beating lets the hummingbird hover, or stay still, in midair. While hovering, the hummingbird sticks its long, slender bill into a flower and uses its long, tubelike tongue to suck up a sweet liquid called nectar. The name *hummingbird*, by the way, came from the low humming sound produced by the bird's rapid wing movement.

What's this chimpanzee doing with the stick in its paw?

He's using the stick as a tool, something scientists at one time thought only people could do. By nature, chimpanzees are curious, and this one figured out how to use the stick as a way of getting a meal. When the chimp pokes the stick into the holes of the termite mound, termites attack the stick by swarming—just as they would with any invader. When the chimp pulls the stick out of the mound, it's covered with an instant insect snack!

Is this raccoon washing its food?

No. But like all raccoons, this one spends a lot of time feeling around in shallow creeks for crayfish, frogs, and other prey. People used to think that raccoons wash their food because the ones that live in captivity have a habit of dipping their dinner in their water bowls. Turning the food over and over in their nimble paws, these captive raccoons seem to be scrubbing it clean. But scientists now think they're just instinctively going through the motions of "finding" their prey the way raccoons in the wild do.

Why is this bird's mouth crisscrossed?

When it comes to picking apart pinecones, a crisscrossed bill is the best tool for the job. Red crossbills, such as the one shown here, use their beaks to pry apart and hold open pinecone scales. Then they reach between the scales with their tongues, snatch the seeds inside, and gulp them down. Part of the finch family of birds, red crossbills live in North America and build their nests in the trees whose pinecones they feed on.

Why is this animal poking its nose into a mound of dirt?

This giant anteater is sniffing out a termite dinner. It will use its sharp, curved claws to slash an opening in this tough termite mound. Then it will flick its long, worm-shaped tongue in and out of the hole, nabbing dozens of the tiny termites with each swipe of its sticky tongue. Some anteaters can flick their 2-foot (61-centimeter) tongues in and out of a termite mound or anthill more than 150 times a minute. Now that's really "fast food"!

How can this big clumsy bear catch slippery fish in all this rushing water?

Alaskan brown bears may *look* big and clumsy, but you'd be surprised at how fast and agile they really are—even when they're fishing for salmon in a rushing stream. Some bears stand on the shore until they spot a silvery red salmon making its way upstream. Then they leap in, trying to land belly down on top of the fish and pin it to the bottom with a paw or their mouth. Other bears like this one wade in to try to snatch the slippery fish as they swim by. Still, even with their sharp claws and quick reflexes, Alaskan brown bears miss more fish than they catch.

If a starfish's body is almost all arms, where is its mouth?

Right smack in the center of its underside. Each of the starfish's five arms has a groove, and where the grooves meet is at its small, circular mouth. Each groove is lined with tiny suckers called tube feet. When the starfish finds a clam, scallop, or oyster, it wraps its arms around the animal's shell and uses the tiny suckers on each arm to get a good grip. With the suckers holding fast to the shell, the starfish uses its arms to force the shell open. Then the starfish pushes its stomach out through its mouth, wrapping its stomach around the prey's body. Slowly, the starfish's stomach digests the prey's tissue.

If bears eat meat, why is this one eating a plant?

Bears *are* meat-eating animals, but they also enjoy many other kinds of food. Fish, ants, grubs, birds' eggs, acorns, berries, fruits, nuts, roots, and, yes, honey all taste good to bears. The animal you see here is the giant panda, considered by many scientists to be

a member of the bear family. Giant pandas eat almost nothing but bamboo, a plant that grows in large forests in western China. These animals are different from other bears in ways that help them eat their special food. Their large teeth are broad and flat—perfect for grinding bamboo leaves and stems. They also have an enlarged wrist bone on their front feet that they use like an extra thumb to grasp the bamboo plants. Because their stomachs do not digest bamboo very well, giant pandas have to eat large amounts of bamboo (up to sixty pounds, or twenty-seven kilograms) a day in order to get the healthful nutrients they need.

Does this sea otter have red whiskers?

Those aren't whiskers at all—they're a "sticky" stumbling block to a meal! When sea otters get hungry, they dive up to 100 feet (30 meters) below the icy waters of the northern Pacific Ocean to look for crabs, shrimp, shellfish, and other forms of sea life. This otter has snagged a sea urchin, a creature with a ball-shaped body covered in movable spines. While floating on its back, the sea otter uses its teeth and paws to pry off enough sea urchin spines so that it can then try to crack the shell for the soft meat inside. And to crack the shell, the floating sea otter often smashes it against a stone that the otter places on its belly for this purpose. If spiny sea urchins are not to the sea otter's taste, it might try shellfish—its favorite snack—instead. The stone-smashing approach also works well on the shells of snails and clams.

Why is this fish spitting?

This archerfish is not really "spitting." Instead, it's using a stream of hard-hitting water to catch a meal. When an archerfish spots an insect crawling on an overhanging leaf, it lines up its body in the water under the insect and takes aim. Then it quickly forces water from its gill chambers into a small groove in the roof of its mouth. It also pushes its tongue up, which narrows the spray of water and makes it squirt out hard and fast. Some of these sharpshooting fish can hit a target more than six feet (nearly two meters) away.

What are these elephants doing in such deep, thick grass?

These elephants look like they're lying down and taking a rest in deep, thick grass, but in fact they're standing in a swamp in Kenya, a country in east-central Africa. Swamps have plenty of the African elephant's favorite foods: grass, small bushes, leaves, roots, bark, branches, fruit, and water plants. And that's what these elephants are doing— feeding on all the swamp plants. A fully grown African elephant, the largest of all land animals, eats about 300 pounds (140 kilograms) of plants and drinks about 40 gallons (150 liters) of water *every day*.

Getting Around

Is this bird walking on water?

Well, almost. With its long legs and toes, claws that are flat and straight, and well-distributed body weight, the African jacana is able to walk delicately over lily pads and other types of floating plants in pools and lakes. The jacana is an excellent swimmer though, and it will dive under the water to escape danger. It feeds on animals and seeds in the water, and sometimes eats fish.

How fast can a cheetah run?

The cheetah can run up to 70 miles (113 kilometers) per hour, at least for short bursts. It is believed to be the fastest mammal on earth. Like any other cat, the African cheetah stalks its prey (gazelles or other small, hoofed animals) by crouching low to the ground and sneaking up as close as possible. Then it jumps up and tries to catch the animal before it can escape. If the animal manages to run away, the cheetah is usually fast enough to overtake it. And when it does, it will knock the animal down with its large paws.

Won't this bug drown underwater?

If it stays under *too* long, yes, it will. But the great diving beetle of Europe spends a good deal of time below water, where it hunts for small amphibians (animals living both on land and in water) and fish. With its flat, streamlined body and oarlike hind legs, this beetle is an excellent diver. After it has been underwater for a while, the beetle comes to the surface, quickly sticks its rear end out of the water, and then dives back down again. This diving action squeezes old air out and draws in fresh air. The air goes in and out of a slit between the end of the beetle's abdomen and the tip of its wing covers. At the same time, the beetle also collects a bubble of extra air that is stored in an airtight space under its wings. This reserve air lets the great diving beetle stay underwater even longer.

Is this penguin swimming on snow?

Actually, it's more like taking a belly sleigh ride. Adélie penguins are best adapted for swimming in the sea, but their short feet, rudderlike tails, streamlined bodies, and flipperlike wings don't help them when they come out of the water to breed. On land, these flightless birds mostly waddle about. But when it is icy, they can speed things up by tobogganing on their bellies, as this penguin is doing. Adélie penguins nest in large colonies around the Antarctic coast, and both males and females help to incubate their eggs (keep them warm and protected). To keep warm themselves, adult Adélie penguins have three waterproof layers of feathers as well as a layer of fat. When they dive underwater for food (mostly tiny animals called *krill*), they can stay below for six minutes because their heartbeat is reduced in response to the coldness of the water and so they need less blood and oxygen.

How far can this ape leap?

The incredibly agile white-handed gibbon, a small Asian ape, can actually launch itself through the trees up to a distance of thirty feet (nine meters). Usually, though, gibbons use their long, powerful arms to swing through the trees, relying on a hand-over-hand motion called *brachiation*. Gibbons sometimes come down from the trees to the ground, where they walk in an upright position.

Can a kangaroo hop very far?

At a slow pace, the red kangaroo can hop 4 to 6 feet (122 to 183 centimeters). But when it needs to move fast, it can travel as far as thirty feet (nine meters) with each hop and reach a speed of over fifty miles (eighty kilometers) per hour—at least, for a short time. This large marsupial, or pouched animal, lives on the dry grasslands of Australia in areas that receive very little rainfall. Sometimes red kangaroos must travel over 150 miles (241 kilometers) just to find water. During the heat of the day, they rest behind rocks or bushes.

Can snakes swim?

Not all snakes can swim. But some, like this banded sea snake, are aquatic, which means they spend their whole lives in the water. With long, bendable bodies and tails used like paddles, sea snakes are good swimmers. Though they need to breathe, sea snakes are able to stay underwater for several minutes before coming up for air. The snakes' nostrils point upward and can be sealed tightly to keep out water. Sea snakes eat fish, which they kill with venom, or poison, stored in their fangs (long, sharp, hollow front teeth connected to glands holding venom).

How does this animal fly?

It looks like it's flying through the air, but this sugar glider of Australia and New Guinea is really gliding from one tree to another on a cushion of air. When a sugar glider leaps from a tree, it extends its front and hind legs, which spread open a membrane of skin called the gliding membrane. As it lands, the animal instantly folds in the membrane so that the extra skin doesn't hamper its movements as it climbs about. Sugar gliders are in the possum family and are marsupials, which means that, like kangaroos, they carry their young in a pouch. Sugar gliders live in trees and feed on sap (liquid flowing through a tree or other plant), nectar (a sweet liquid in flowers), and fruit.

Why do these spiders have strings stuck to them?

This is a triple-exposure photo (three different photographs shot closely together and shown together here) of *one* jumping spider in midleap. The string is really a thread of silk that the half-inch-long (one-centimeter-long) spider sends out as a kind of safety line. Jumping spiders live mostly in the tropics and hunt during the day. They have no trouble spotting their prey (insects) since they have four pairs of eyes, with each pair seeing different-sized images. Jumping spiders usually don't miss their mark when they jump with their eight legs anyway. They can often leap up to forty times their body length. For a boy or girl to do the same, he or she would have to jump about 160 feet (49 meters) in one leap!

Is this baby hitching a ride on its mother's back?

Yes, it is. On Madagascar, an island in the West Indian Ocean, ring-tailed lemurs live in groups and travel the forest together in search of such food as fruit, leaves, and flowers. When a baby is born, it clings at first to its mother's belly as she moves about. But after two weeks, the baby lemur rides on the mother's back. At three weeks, it will start climbing on its own, and at four weeks it needs to be with its mother only for nursing and sleeping. Mothers of this species will help care for other lemur babies and will also adopt orphans (babies without parents). Fathers also help take care of the young. Lemurs are very agile and can climb the tallest trees, though they do spend some of their time on the ground to get a drink of water, find more food, or simply play.

What is the gazelle in front doing?

The Thomson's gazelle, or Tommy, that you see leaping out in front through the air is actually doing something called "stotting," which is a four-footed hop. Tommies live on the plains of Africa, and at only two feet (sixty-one centimeters) tall they are prey to many large meat eaters. They stott when they are alarmed, holding their head and tail up, and young Tommies also stott when they're at play. Tommies can make leaps of up to 4½ feet (1.4 meters). They do so to clear ditches but *not* to jump over tall objects such as fences or rocks—unless they have no choice. These graceful gazelles also wag their tails a lot. In fact, newborns wag their tails before they can even move their legs.

Getting the Message

What's this rhinoceros saying?

He could be saying, "Keep away from me." Black rhinoceroses have a pretty good "vocabulary." They can grunt, growl, and squeak, and they make a kind of puffing snort when they are angry or beginning to charge at an animal they consider a threat. When a cow (female) is ready to mate, she and the bull (male) sniff each other around the mouth and often make gurgling sounds. With the exception of when they are mating or caring for their young, rhinos are usually alone, and males will aggressively defend their territories. The African black rhino, by the way, is no more black than the white rhino. For both grayish-toned animals, skin color depends on pigmentation (the effect created by coloring substances in the cells or tissues of animals or plants) and on the mud they wallow in to keep their skin protected.

Is this mouse making a lot of noise?

As much as he can. In the darkness of the night, grasshoppper mice come out of their underground nests to eat, and one of their favorite foods is grasshoppers. While looking for a meal, male grasshopper mice take time out to stand on their back legs, lean their heads back, and make high-pitched sounds lasting several seconds. The females make these sounds less often, and when they do, the sounds are less than a second in length. Grasshopper mice live alone in dry open areas in the United States and Mexico, and are very aggressive toward other members of their species. It's believed that the sounds they make are to let other mice know where they are and to mark their territory.

Are these birds singing together?

With throats opened wide and beaks pointed skyward, these two Japanese cranes are singing a duet, or unison call, which they use as a territorial warning. Other birds can hear their calls from as far as two miles (three kilometers) away. In Japan, these cranes are symbols of happiness and love, because the birds stay with the same mate for life.

Cranes also dance a lot. They leap in the air with their wings stretched out fully, inviting their mates to dance with them. Often they dance as part of their mating ritual. And if one bird starts to dance, it frequently starts a chain reaction of all flock members doing the same.

Why is this chimpanzee smiling?

The chimp isn't smiling—it's actually baring its teeth as a threatening gesture. From the time they're young, male chimpanzees have to determine what their rank in the chimpanzee community will be. They do this by charging through the trees in the African forests where they live, throwing sticks, pulling down branches and swinging them around, and stamping their feet on the ground. They try to look big and strong, and the more impressive their display is, the higher their ranking will be. On occassion, females will also make such displays. Chimpanzees have other ways of communicating, too, such as making different cries and touching, kissing, and stroking one another.

What are these animals whispering?

They're not whispering—they're nuzzling. When hoary marmots meet other members of their family group, they greet each other affectionately, often rubbing noses and grooming each other's thick coats of fur. These North American animals also have another way of communicating, which they use to warn each other if enemies such as coyotes or golden eagles are nearby. They stand up and make loud, earsplitting screams that send all the other members of the colony scurrying for cover—and often send the would-be predator on its way, too.

Why does the humpback whale "sing"?

Scientists aren't sure if the rare humpback whale sings out of sheer joy or whether it does so for another reason. Most likely, the humpback whale sings as a means of finding and communicating with others of its species and as a means of keeping the group together. This is especially important for animals that make regular migrations (long-distance travels) in dark waters between equatorial and polar seas. In the entire animal kingdom, the humpback whale sings the longest and most varied songs, which can carry underwater for distances of over 100 miles (161 kilometers).

Why is this monkey's mouth wide open?

Some monkeys, like this black howler monkey, live in large social groups, but they don't like neighboring groups of howlers to come into their territory. So every morning, each group of howlers will open their mouths wide and make loud calls to let other groups know where they are. They also howl at night sometimes and when there is danger. Howling is a good means of communication for animals who dwell in dense South American forests, where it is easier to hear than to see.

Who is this moose calling to?

When a male moose is courting a female, he calls to her quietly and rhythmically, over and over again. The female also makes soft, rhythmic sounds and moves her jaws up and down. The male walks toward the female slowly, with his body stretched out, and sniffs her. Moose generally only have one mate. If the male sees a rival, he may make a loud call and then chase him away. The moose are the largest members of the deer family, and they live in North America.

Why do wolves howl?

Wolves, like this Mexican gray wolf, live together in groups called packs that have one or more families and sometimes other individuals. Wolves often howl on their own or in chorus with members of their pack to let other wolf packs nearby know of their presence. This helps to avoid conflict over territorial boundaries and also helps to promote a closeness within the group. Wolves are social animals and are much more peaceful than was once believed. The pack is well organized, and members often hunt and bring down prey together. The two oldest wolves, called the Alpha male and female, usually lead the pack. The other wolves know that the Alpha male and female are in charge because the two hold their heads and tails higher than any other members of the pack.

Is this zebra talking to anyone?

This Burchell's, or plains, zebra of Africa is letting out a warning call to other nearby zebras because an enemy is approaching. Like all animals that are preyed upon by other animals, zebras find ways to protect themselves. They live in family groups and alert each other of danger by either calling out or running away from the rest of the herd, which prompts the others to do the same. During the night, one or more zebras will stay awake to stand guard. If a female (mare) zebra is about to have a baby, the male (stallion) will stay with her to protect her. When the herd is threatened, all the zebras travel closely together, with a high-ranking male in the lead and another stallion traveling at the back to defend the group.

Why is this animal standing on its hind legs?

Black-tailed prairie dogs stand on their hind legs to keep a lookout for prairie badgers and other enemies that may be approaching the entrances to their elaborate underground tunnels. And if an enemy comes by, they warn the members of the colony by making a barking sound. That's why they're called "dogs," even though they're really in the squirrel family. Prairie dogs also stand up when they greet each other. These animals live in colonies made up of many individual family groups and make their homes in the central part of the United States.

Staying Alive

Why is this owl holding out its wings?

For the same reason that a cat arches its back: It's trying to make itself look bigger. Like cats and many other animals, this long-eared owl knows that the bigger it looks, the better its chance of warding off an enemy. But it probably didn't have much luck fooling the photographer!

Why does this lizard have flaps of skin sticking up around its neck?

The flaps are part of this Australian frilled lizard's survival "strategy." When it first senses trouble, the lizard will try to escape by sprinting across the ground and scurrying up a tree. As it flees, the skin around its neck is folded over its back and shoulders like a cape. But if an enemy keeps up the chase, the lizard will suddenly spin around, open its mouth wide, and fully extend its neck frill with a dramatic flair. If this "frill thrill" doesn't do the trick, the lizard will step boldly forward, sway back and forth, whip its tail around, and let out a low, angry hiss. Most predators don't stick around to find out what comes next. What they don't know is that this tough-acting lizard is really harmless. And there is one other reason why the Australian frilled lizard extends its flaps—to attract a mate.

What's been nibbling on this leaf?

What leaf? Look closer, and you'll see that this "leaf" has legs, a head, and antennae. It's actually an Asian leaf insect, one of many kinds of insects that can fool predators by looking like leaves, sticks, flowers, or other plant parts. Some of these disguises come complete with leaf "veins," brown "fungus" spots, twig "buds," and other realistic features. And many plant look-alikes even act the part. For example, some kinds of leaf insects sway back and forth like leaves blown by a breeze. And when an enemy gets too close to an oak beauty moth caterpillar (see photo lower right), the insect freezes in a convincing "twig position."

How far can this skunk spray?

It's a good idea to keep your distance when you spy a striped skunk like the one shown here. Even if you were ten feet (three meters) away, this little skunk could hit you with a mist of its oily, yellow, very stinky spray. Luckily, a striped skunk usually gives a warning before it sprays. First, it may stamp its feet, bristle its tail, arch its back, and shake its head from side to side. Then it may curve the rear part of its body forward and raise its tail. Finally, it sprays. The spray shoots out from two tiny rounded tips under the tail, which are connected to glands that produce the smelly musk. The spray not only stinks, but it can also cause the victim's eyes and nostrils to burn. And as if that weren't enough, the spray can cause a terrible upset stomach.

Why did these animals form a circle?

These adult musk-oxen have circled up to protect themselves and their young from a wolf attack. Standing shoulder to shoulder with their sharp horns in clear view, these 800-pound (298-kilogram) mammals create an impressive wall of defense. With their young clustered safely inside, the adults take turns trying to drive away their attackers. They lunge forward, lower their heads, and try to gore the wolves with their razor-sharp horns. In most battles, the huddled, massive musk-oxen win.

Did this fish cover itself in seaweed?

The colorful bits of "seaweed" you see covering this fish are actually little flaps of skin on its bumpy body. When you look like a clump of seaweed, as this scorpionfish, enemies are probably not going to notice you. Also, prey are not likely to notice a predator that has such an effective disguise as the scorpionfish. Some sea creatures walk or swim within inches of these well-disguised fish without realizing they're in big trouble. And when an animal gets within reach, the scorpionfish springs into action. It snaps open its oversized mouth, sucks in the unlucky animal, and gulps it down. Before the "dust" settles, this tricky trapper is back on the bottom, lying in wait again.

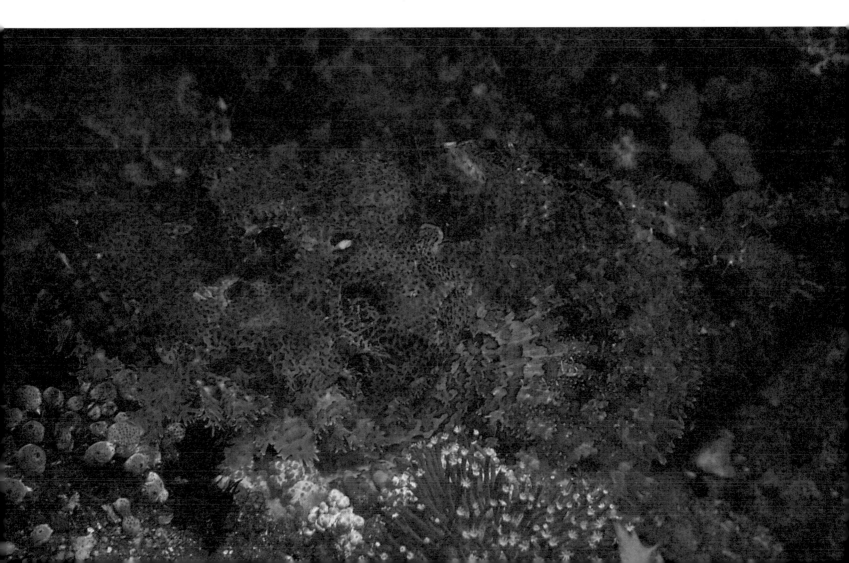

Does this butterfly have an eye on its wings?

The "eye" that you see on the hind wing of this owl butterfly isn't an eye at all. It just *looks* like an eye. The owl butterfly has the same "eye" marking on each of its hind wings. Some experts think the bold, bright spots on the hind wings help focus a predator's attention on the tail and away from the butterfly's head. This "trick" can help save a butterfly's life. A butterfly can lose its antennae or entire head if a predator tries to grab a butterfly's head. But if a predator takes a chunk out of the hind wing, the butterfly has a better chance of surviving. Another possible benefit of these butterfly "eyes" is that from a distance they look like the eyes of a much larger creature. That may help scare off the butterfly's enemies.

How does this slow-moving sloth protect itself from its enemies?

Definitely not by running away. At its fastest, this three-toed sloth can reach speeds of only about one and a quarter miles (two kilometers) per hour—and that's in the trees, where it's adapted to spending most of its time. On the ground, sloths have a tough time getting around. Their back legs, built for climbing and clinging to branches, can't support their weight, so the animals can only drag themselves along with their front legs. If frightened or attacked, sloths can do some damage with their sharp claws. But a sloth's best defense may be the fact that the animal just doesn't attract attention. That's because sloths don't move around very much at all. In fact, for about fifteen hours each day, sloths just sleep.

Why do these deer have spots?

Sprinkles of white spots on their fur help these Axis deer blend into the background of grasses, brush, and the natural, sun-dappled floor of their outdoor home in India. This makes it harder for prowling predators to "spot" the spotted deer. And when enemies get too close, the spotted deer are off like a flash, sometimes reaching a speed of forty miles (sixty-four kilometers) an hour in the chase for life. Spots are especially helpful to baby Axis deer, called fawns. Enemies can easily miss the young animals, which lie very still for long periods while their mothers go off to feed. And since a newborn fawn has no scent, a predator can come very close to it without even knowing it's there.

Is this millipede curled up for a snooze?

Nine inches (twenty-three centimeters) long, the East African giant millipede you see here is not snoozing at all. In fact, it's wide awake and keenly alert, protecting itself from attack. If surprised or frightened, these insect relatives coil up like a watch spring so that only their tough outer covering is exposed. They also give off a smelly, poisonous liquid from stink glands on their legs. The ooze is so stinky and distasteful that most enemies leave them alone. By the way, did you know that the word *millipede* means "thousand-footed"?

Oddly enough, no millipede has more than 115 pairs of legs, or 230 all together.

How does this fish turn itself into a ball of spines?

When threatened, this porcupinefish (also called the spiny puffer) swimming in the waters off Panama's northern coast quickly puffs itself up by filling its stomach with water or air. This causes the strong, sharp spines lying flat on the porcupinefish's body to stand up. Though not poisonous, these spines can sting and wound an attacker.

Wild & Crazy Colors

What kind of monkey has such a colorful face?

This bright-faced baboon is a male mandrill of West Africa. Scientists think that the colors of a male mandrill become brighter or bolder when it gets angry or feels threatened. These brighter colors are a signal that warns other males to keep their distance. Mandrills also use color to back down from a fight. When retreating from a bigger and brighter male, the loser will expose its two blue rump patches. This sends a message to the big guy that says, "Please don't hurt me—I'm leaving!"

Why are these blue things scattered all over the ground?

These blue trinkets belong to a male satin bowerbird. The color blue is irresistible to these Australian birds. They collect all kinds of blue stuff—from flowers to bits of glass to just plain trash. Then they carefully place their trinkets in and around a special "hut," called a bower, that they build out of grass. Female bowerbirds inspect the bower and its decorations. If a female approves of the male's handiwork, she will mate with him and build her nest nearby.

Why are these frogs so colorful?

Bright red eyes, orange feet, and a green body help the gaudy leaf frog (above left) stay alive. When resting, these colorful little frogs do their best to stay out of sight. They close their eyes to hide the red and keep their body tucked tight. But if disturbed, they flash their red eyes at their attackers and expose their orange feet. These bright colors often startle a would-be attacker and give the little frogs enough time to hop to safety.

The arrow-poison frog (above right) sends a different message with its colorful markings and striking patterns. It has poisons in its skin that can kill an enemy in seconds. Its colors and patterns are a warning that says, "Leave me alone."

Why are these flamingos partly pink?

Whoever first said "you are what you eat" probably wasn't talking about flamingos. But this saying may be truer for flamingos than it is for people! A flamingo's diet of tiny water plants and animals is full of substances called *carotenoids*. These substances cause flamingos' feathers to turn pink—and the more carotenoids their diets contain, the pinker they get. (You eat carotenoids, too, whenever you eat carrots, beets, and certain other vegetables. But you don't eat enough to make you change color.) In captivity, flamingos often lose their pink color because their diets don't contain enough carotenoids. To make the birds more colorful, zookeepers often add carotenoid-rich substances to the flamingos' food.

Why is this beetle so shiny?

No one really knows why some insects, like this gold scarab beetle, are so "flashy." Some scientists think the shimmering colors may scare away enemies. Others think the bright colors may actually help the beetles hide in shiny foliage. But what scientists *do* know for sure is how these beetles glimmer in the light.

If you looked at this scarab beetle under a microscope, you would see tiny bumps, pits, ridges, and notches all over its body. When light strikes this uneven surface, it bounces off in all directions—just as it does when light strikes the grooves of a compact disc (CD). This bouncing light, called iridescence, makes the beetle shine and shimmer. Iridescence can also make some beetles look like they're changing colors all the time: green or gold one minute, blue or purple the next.

Why do zebras have stripes?

Because of their distinctive stripes, zebras at first glance look like they'd be an easy mark for lions and other natural enemies. But many scientists think that the bold black and white stripes of a zebra might actually help to protect it. Zebras live in herds, and all those stripes may make it hard for enemies to focus on any one zebra. So having a pattern that stands out may be the best way for a zebra *not* to stand out in a crowd!

Why does this lizard have a bright blue tail?

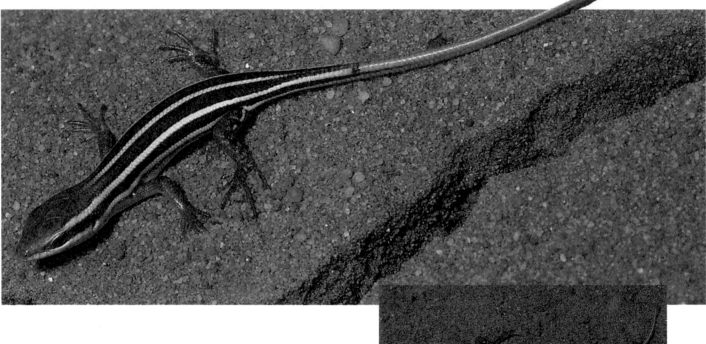

The blue-tailed skink's tail could save its life! The bright color catches the attention of enemies like birds and snakes. But when an enemy goes after a skink's tail, the tail breaks off in the enemy's mouth. The blue tail wiggles and twitches for a few seconds, providing just enough of a distraction to let the little lizard get away. After losing a tail, most skinks can eventually regrow them, although the new tail is usually a little shorter and stubbier than the original.

Why does this bird look so dressed up?

The one-wattled cassowary of Indonesia looks *very* dressed up with the bright blue color under its head and bright red color along its neck. And these flashy colors help attract a mate. The rest of this large, rather shy bird is covered in bristly, brownish-black feathers, with gray legs and feet. About 5 feet (1 ½ meters) tall, the cassowary is a flightless but fast-sprinting bird related to the ostrich. It's also a real "bonehead." That's because its head is crowned with a bony crest, a built-in "helmet" that may provide protection as the bird moves through dense jungle plants. But being "boneheaded" and flightless isn't all that's unusual about the cassowary. It's also a great swimmer, unlike most other ostrichlike birds. And when it's time to raise young, it's the father that incubates the eggs (keeps them warm and protected) and guards the chicks.

Is this monkey blushing?

No. Uakaris don't blush. Bright red faces and heads are normal for these South American monkeys. For many years, people thought these rare treetop climbers turned bright red when they became angry or spent too much time in the sun. But now experts think these fruit eaters stay bright red most of the time and only turn pale pink when they're sick.

Animal Oddities

How many suckers does this octopus have on its arms?

Would you guess dozens? Hundreds? How about a couple of *thousand*! The common octopus, like the one shown, usually has 240 suckers on each of its 8 arms, giving it a total of—well, *you* figure it out! An octopus is in complete control of all of its suckers. Whether they're gripping a rock or a prey animal such as a crab, the suckers "stick" with amazing strength. But if the octopus needs to make a quick getaway, it can let go in an instant.

Why does this insect have such a long neck?

It's not actually a neck—it's a long, stretched-out head! No one is exactly sure what purpose this strange feature serves on the well-named giraffe weevil. Scientists *do* know that the giraffe weevil has an unusual habit of rolling the edges of leaves to make a little hideaway for its eggs. A female will cut the edge of a leaf with her jaws until it is hanging by only a thread. Then she rolls it up to make a little barrel, where she lays a single egg. She does this, leaf after leaf, until all her eggs are laid.

What does this creature have sticking out of its head?

Those frilly plumes are gills, special organs that absorb oxygen from the water. Like most amphibians (animals living both on land and in water), this crested newt will only need gills for part of its life. As it changes into an adult, the gills will disappear and internal lungs will develop, allowing the newt to breathe air and live on land. Although crested newts often live on land for several years, they always return to the water to breed. And during the mating season, the males grow a showy crest, stretching from its head to its tail.

Do warthogs have warts?

The warthog may not be a great beauty, but it is one animal that lives up to its name. Warthogs have three pairs of large warts on their faces between the tusks and the eyes. This grass-eating roamer of sub-Saharan Africa's wide open spaces might just as easily have been called an "elephant hog" because it is a pig with tusks. These pointy tusks may grow as long as two feet (sixty-one centimeters), though the warthog prefers to run from a larger enemy rather than use its tusks to stand and fight.

What monster is this?

When photographed this close up, the bug-eyed, orange-lipped tropical katydid from South America *does* look like a spiky-headed monster. But most katydids are just two inches (five centimeters) long. That's about the size of your little pinky finger! Experts aren't sure why the katydid, which is a type of grasshopper, has such flashy colors and spiffy spines. But some scientists think the bright colors may scare away enemies. And the spiky spines may look so sharp and fierce that an enemy wouldn't even try to gulp down the insect. By the way, can you guess why these insects are called katydids? The answer is that some males have a mating call that sounds like "KAY-tih-did" chirped over and over again.

Why do these animals have such big noses?

If you're a male proboscis monkey (right) or a male elephant seal (below), the bigger your snout, the better. That's because the bigger the nose, the better the chances of winning a mate. During the breeding season, both of these super-snouted mammals make distinctive mating calls. The proboscis monkey makes a loud honking noise, while the elephant seal makes a deep trumpeting sound. Their noses act like amplifiers, with the biggest noses making the loudest calls. Scientists think that females are attracted to those males that have the biggest snouts and make the loudest calls. No wonder the males like to "blow their own horns"!

How does a platypus use its bill?

A platypus's bill—actually a snout covered with moist, rubbery skin—is a food-finding "machine." As it swims along stream and river bottoms, this odd Australian mammal uses its super-sensitive snout to probe into mud and gravel for insects, snails, crayfish, and other small animals. But platypuses don't just feel around for their food—they also use a special "sixth sense." Their sensitive snouts are equipped with an organ that can detect the weak electrical currents produced when an animal's muscles contract. By sensing these currents, a platypus has a better shot of zeroing in on its prey.

Is this a frog or a fish?

Although its bulging eyes, huge head, and slimy skin may make you think of a tadpole, this odd-looking creature is really a fish. So why is it out of the water, clinging to a branch? Because it's a mudskipper—and unlike most fish, it can get oxygen from *both* air and water. In addition to gills, it has special membranes (very thin skin layers) lining the back of its mouth and throat that allow it to breathe air.

Mudskippers get their name from the way they use their hind fins to get around in the mud. During low tide, hundreds of these fish "skip" along mudflats in Africa and Asia, skimming algae (large group of plants without roots or flowers) as well as microscopic plants from the water.

Is the bigger animal a dragon, and is that its baby on its back?

Although the bigger animal here may look something like a dragon, it is a rather gentle creature called a marine iguana. A type of large lizard, the marine iguana lives in the Galápagos Islands, located in the Pacific Ocean west of South America. Like many of the creatures of the Galápagos, the marine iguana is one of the most unusual animals on earth. It is the only lizard that is truly at home in the sea, and it is the only one that eats sea algae, especially seaweed. (Algae are a large group of plants without roots or flowers.) You can get a sense of the marine iguana's size from the smaller lizard perched on its back. The tiny lava lizard can take a fine sunbath atop its larger cousin when the marine iguana visits dry land.

Why is this bird hanging upside down?

It's amazing what some animals will do for attention. Just ask this male Emperor of Germany's bird of paradise living in New Guinea. Like other birds of paradise, he'll go all out to attract a female's attention. Hanging upside down and shaking his feathers, he shows off his bright green upper body plumage (cover of feathers). If a female bird of paradise likes his performance, she may choose him for a mate.

What causes the eyes of this animal to shine in the dark?

It's all done with "mirrors." This small, catlike creature is called a civet, or civet cat, and it has a special surface at the back of its eyes that helps it hunt at night. Like a mirror, this surface reflects light, causing the civet's eyes to shine. The reflected light helps nighttime animals like the civet to see better in the dark.

Don't Mess With Me

Why are these cats snarling at each other?

Cats jealously protect their territories from outsiders and will fight them to chase them off. Here, it seems a jaguar outsider (which one is hard to say) has barked up the wrong tree. Jaguars will fight fiercely if cornered or disturbed, and these two seem ready to square off if one doesn't back down soon. The largest New World (Western Hemisphere) cats, jaguars are found from the U.S.-Mexico border to Patagonia, at the southern tip of South America. You can tell a jaguar by its spots. Groups of black spots are arranged like flower petals around a black spot at the center.

Why is one beetle flipping another up in the air?

These two male stag beetles are fighting for the right to mate with the female beetle lingering nearby. The stronger male is using his large jaws to heave the weaker one up in the air before tossing him over his back. Some types of male stag beetles have these oversized jaws, which look like the antlers on the heads of male deer, or stags. That is why they are called "stag" beetles. These antlerlike jaws may be nearly as large as the beetle's entire body. A pinch from a stag beetle, sometimes called a pinching bug, can draw blood from a human.

What fish has such sharp, nasty-looking teeth?

This is the red piranha, one of the fiercest fish in the world. Up to a foot (thirty centimeters) long, this meat eater lives in the Amazon River of South America. It uses its razor-sharp teeth and scissorlike bite to tear large chunks out of its prey. Piranhas often attack in large numbers. Some scientists think they are more dangerous than sharks, though piranhas seldom attack humans. Usually, piranhas eat other fish. But they also can tear all the flesh off of large animals that wander into the waters where piranhas live. They finish their deadly work in a matter of minutes, leaving only bones behind.

Are these walruses trying to stab each other with their tusks?

No. Rarely will a walrus use its tusks to try to wound seriously or kill another walrus. Most walruses settle their arguments by sparring, using their tusks to poke, prod, or threaten each other. But a walrus *will* use its tusks as serious weapons to fight off polar bears. And though walruses generally do not attack people, a wounded animal might use its tusks to do damage to hunters and their boats. Far more often, however, the tusks serve a nonviolent purpose, acting as hooks to help the walrus pull itself out of the water onto the ice. This mammal of the Arctic and northern ocean waters is the only type of seal that has tusks. They are actually upper teeth that point downward and may grow thirty-nine inches (ninety-nine centimeters) long.

Do all sharks eat people?

All sharks are meat eaters, but very few sharks are *people* eaters. The largest of all sharks—in fact, the largest of all fishes—is the forty-foot-long (twelve-meter-long) whale shark above, which feeds only on plankton (tiny sea animals and plants) and small fish. Still, all sharks should be considered dangerous by any person who takes to the water, even though only about one tenth of all sharks, or twenty-five species, have been known to attack humans. In the past, it was thought that sharks never stopped feeding and would attack any human immediately. Now scientists know that they can go for weeks or even months without eating, living off the oil stored in their liver. What scientists still don't know is why sharks attack at some times but not at others. The sand tiger shark seen on the right lives in the Mediterranean Sea, Atlantic Ocean, and the waters off South Africa. About twelve feet (four meters) long, the sand tiger shark is sometimes called the "wolf of the sea" because it is so fierce and often hunts in packs like wolves.

Who's winning this battle?

Not the snake, that's for sure. About sixteen inches (forty-one centimeters) long, the common Indian mongoose is more than a match for most of the snakes it meets. That's because the mongoose is very fast on its feet. It dodges and pounces with lightning speed. These quick, dancelike movements enable the animal to kill snakes as large and dangerous as cobras. The mongoose darts toward a snake's neck, finally breaking it with a very strong bite. Mongooses have to be careful, though, because they have no special protection against the snakes' poison.

Does a lionfish roar?

Although you won't hear it make a sound, the lionfish is no pussycat. This inhabitant of warm-water seas swims boldly out in the open, with its bright pattern of color saying "keep away" to other fish. If an undersea neighbor is unlucky enough to cause a fuss, the lionfish spreads its fins fully and points its dorsal, or back, fin spines right at the other fish. These spines are needle-sharp and give off a poison. If the other fish still does not back off, the lionfish will attack with its spines. Lionfish have even been known to attack skin divers!

The
Great
Cover-Up

Do polar bears ever get cold?

Rarely. A thick, dense coat of hair, rolls of fat called blubber under the skin, and furry feet are three features that help polar bears stay cozy in the frigid world of the Arctic. If you looked at a polar bear hair under a microscope, you'd see a hollow, transparent tube. A polar bear looks white because the colorless hairs reflect all wavelengths of light and at the same time allow sunlight to strike the polar bear's coal-black skin. The dark skin acts like a sponge that soaks up heat. And the hollow hairs, which are filled with air, trap the heat in the same way that panes of glass in a greenhouse trap sunlight. Polar bears also have four inches (ten centimeters) of blubber under their skin to keep the cold out. And they have thick fur on the undersides of their feet that not only keeps their toes toasty, but also keeps them from slipping on ice.

Why is this hippo covered in mud?

Taking a mud bath is a great way for this 4-ton (3.6-metric-ton) hippopotamus to keep cool in the hot, African sun. A roll in the mud can also get rid of insect pests, keep the hippo's skin moist and protect it from sun damage, and ease the pain of scratches, stings, and bug bites. Besides cool mud baths, these huge mammals have another "natural" protection for their two-inch-thick (five-centimeter-thick) hides. It's a reddish oil that comes up through the pores, or small openings, in their skin and spreads out over it. People once thought that hippos were "sweating blood." But experts now know that the oil is special, helping to hold in moisture, kill germs, and heal wounds.

Is this animal covered in armor?

Spanish explorers to southern America thought so. Hundreds of years ago, when they first found this animal, explorers from Spain thought that its hard shell looked like armor. So they called it *armadillo,* which means "little armored animal" in Spanish. Although it looks like a little armored dinosaur, this nine-banded armadillo is a mammal just like you. Its shell has nine narrow bands of skin-covered, bony plates that help protect it from brambles and branches as well as from foxes, wolves, and other predators. But armadillos do have a few soft spots, including their belly and the fleshy tip of their noses. When danger threatens, armadillos can roll into a tight ball or curl up enough to cover these unprotected body parts. They can also use their powerful, curved claws and strong front feet to dig a tunnel quickly and disappear right before an attacker's eyes.

How can this snake climb trees?

This green python of Australia and New Guinea is scaling the heights—literally. You have hands, legs, and feet to help you climb, but snakes have something you don't have—wide belly scales connected to strong muscles. They also have a flexible rib cage, with more than 200 ribs. When a snake like this green python climbs a tree, these belly scales work in sync with the ribs to pull and push the snake up the tree. The scales and ribs in the rear dig in as the upper body pulls itself up and forward. Then the rear scales inch up, while the head and upper body hold tight. Some snakes also have a very strong, grasping tail that can help grip tree trunks and branches as they climb.

Are these animals both porcupines?

Although it looks like a miniature porcupine, the prickly mammal eating an earthworm (see photo above left) is really a hedgehog. Both porcupines and hedgehogs have spiny "armor," but the hedgehog's spines are much shorter and stiffer than a porcupine's long quills (see photo above right). Porcupines and hedgehogs also have different ways of protecting themselves from enemies. If a hedgehog spies a predator, it immediately curls up into a tight, spiny ball, tucking its head and legs inside. Most predators don't even try to pry open the prickly ball of spines. But porcupines use a different trick. A porcupine's sharp, barbed quills are loosely attached to its body and tail. When a predator brushes against the animal, the quills can come off and lodge in the predator's flesh. Porcupines can also smack an enemy with their quill-filled tails.

What's wrong with the horned sheep's fur?

This adult Dall's sheep is shedding its thick winter coat and replacing it with a cooler, shorter summer coat. Dall's sheep live on the mountains of Alaska, the Yukon Territory, and British Columbia. In winter, they need a thick "overcoat" to protect them from the fierce winds and cold, snowy weather of their homes high in the mountains. But once the days start getting longer and warmer, the sheep shed their heavy fur, clump by clump. Why don't all these Dall's sheep look ragged? The smaller sheep in this photo are too young to shed. They were born in early spring and will not shed for another year.

What is so special about the wings of butterflies?

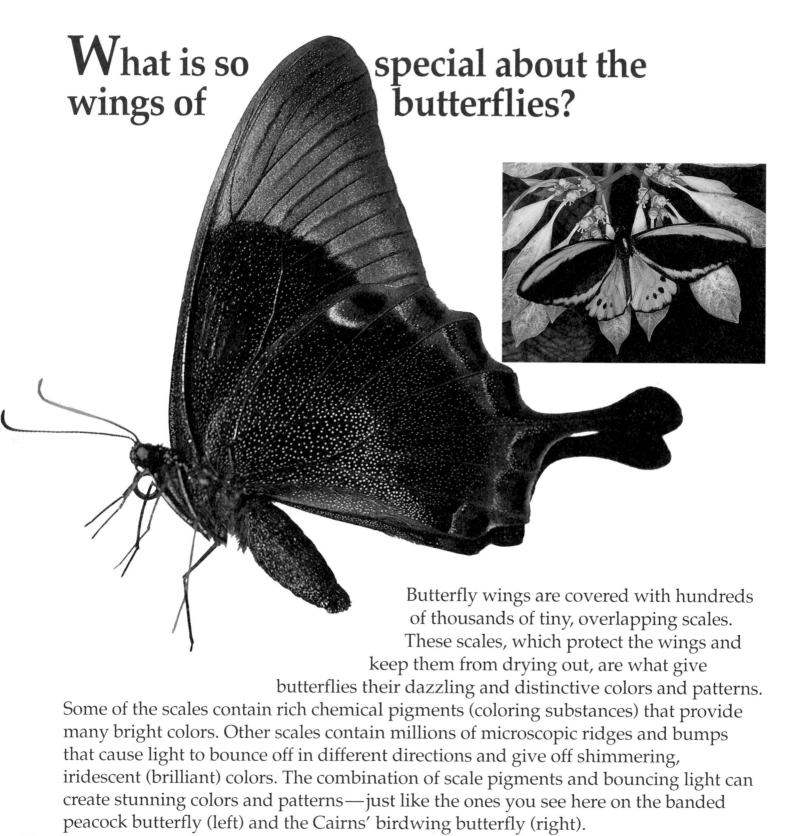

Butterfly wings are covered with hundreds of thousands of tiny, overlapping scales. These scales, which protect the wings and keep them from drying out, are what give butterflies their dazzling and distinctive colors and patterns. Some of the scales contain rich chemical pigments (coloring substances) that provide many bright colors. Other scales contain millions of microscopic ridges and bumps that cause light to bounce off in different directions and give off shimmering, iridescent (brilliant) colors. The combination of scale pigments and bouncing light can create stunning colors and patterns—just like the ones you see here on the banded peacock butterfly (left) and the Cairns' birdwing butterfly (right).

How can a seal survive in such icy water?

Under this harp seal's silvery gray skin lies a thick layer of fat called blubber. It helps to keep the harp seal warm in the frequently frigid waters of the White Sea north of Russia, as well as off the east coast of Greenland and the north coast of Newfoundland. Harp seals also have a two-layered coat: a layer of coarse outer fur, called guard hairs, and a layer of short, dense underfur. The underfur traps small air bubbles against the animals' skin. These bubbles help to hold heat close to the body and also keep the skin dry. The stiff guard hairs aren't heat retainers as much as skin protectors. They keep a seal's skin from getting cut and bruised when the animal hauls itself onto ice floes or rocky shores.

When harp seals are first born, they enter their frozen world with a thick coat of silky white fur. But in a matter of weeks, they shed their fluffy white coat and grow a light gray coat that makes them look a lot more like adults.

What kind of lizard is climbing this tree?

This may *look* like a lizard, but in fact it's an insect-eating mammal called a pangolin. Unlike most mammals, pangolins are covered with hard, overlapping scales instead of hair. These sharp-edged scales look like the woody scales of a pinecone and grow from a thick, underlying layer of skin. Only the animals' soft undersides are hairy. To protect these "soft spots," pangolins curl up into a tight ball. Only strong-jawed predators such as lions and hyenas can unroll this scaly ball. And sometimes they pay a price for their meal if they get cut by the scales, which the pangolin can move with its muscles in a limited way.

Animal Antics

Why are these monkeys taking a bath in such snowy weather?

Because the water is actually *very* warm. These Japanese macaques are enjoying a dip in a hot spring pool, which is a kind of a natural "hot tub." A hot spring often forms when ground water seeps below the surface, is heated by molten rock, and then bubbles up as steam or hot water, forming pools or streams. Unlike other monkeys, which live in warm climates, Japanese macaques live in the cold, snowy mountains of northern Japan. That's why they're often called snow monkeys. Their extra-thick coats help them keep the chill away—and so does an occasional plunge into a hot spring like this one.

Why is this whale jumping out of the water?

No one knows for sure why whales, like this twenty-seven-foot (eight-meter) female killer whale, hurl themselves into the air and then fall back to the sea with a mighty splash. But some experts think this behavior, called *breaching*, may help killer whales drive and eventually corral such prey as squid, seals, walruses, salmon, and other fish. The acrobatic jumps of the graceful, powerful killer whale may also help it communicate with and even "show off" to other killer whales.

How did this animal get stuck in a plastic can?

Deliberately. This hermit crab is just using the blue plastic container for protection. Hermit crabs don't have shells of their own, so they use empty seashells—or, in this case, a thrown-away plastic container—to cover their soft bodies. When a hermit crab outgrows its "adopted" shell, it moves into a larger one. Gripping the inside with its four rear legs and using its four front legs (behind the claws) for walking, a hermit crab carries its "armor" wherever it goes.

Why is this buffalo trying to push over the tree?

Weighing up to 3,000 pounds (1,400 kilograms) and growing up to 12 ½ feet (nearly 4 meters) long, a fully grown American buffalo bull certainly has the strength to topple some small trees. But that's not what this particular bull is doing. It's mock-sparring, or play-fighting, and it's using the tree as an opponent. Sometimes, too, the smell of another male buffalo is on the tree, and that prompts the bull to horn it. The rut you see in this tree was probably made by many buffalo bull horns. During mating season, male buffalo will clash head on against each other for the right to mate.

Are these fish kissing?

Well, maybe. These fish *are* pressing their lips together, and they *are* called kissing gouramis. No one knows for sure why gouramis do this. Perhaps a smooch on the lips may be one way male and female gouramis court. Kissing may also be a sign of aggression, as big gouramis seem to pick on smaller ones occasionally by "kissing" the smaller fish on their flanks.

Why are these hares boxing?

The sparring you see here is probably part of courtship and mating in the spring when hares like these two are most active. Hares in springtime often thump the ground with their strong hind legs and twist their bodies as they leap high into the air. Sometimes they rear up on their hind paws and swat each other with their front paws. Have you ever heard the expression "mad as a March hare"? Well, those words say a lot about what these "March hares" are probably doing—jostling for the right to mate!

Do all animals yawn?

No, but a lot of animals do, including birds, mammals, and fish. Just like you, animals yawn when they're tired. But scientists think one purpose of yawning may be to help animals—and people—perk up. The extra air animals take in when they yawn may provide a surge of oxygen to their brains, making them more alert. This could explain why predators often yawn before going hunting.

How can this spider breathe underwater?

This swamp spider of the Dolomedes family can breathe underwater by wrapping itself in a thin coat of air bubble, made up of tiny, tightly connected air bubbles, that it holds closely to its legs and body. Found in the United States, this spider will crawl along the underwater stalk in hopes of surprising and catching its prey, including water insects, tadpoles, and very small fish. But the "air suit" will not last long, so the spider must work fairly quickly to catch a meal.

Is this animal dancing?

It may look like dancing to you, but it's quite natural for this animal to move along the ground in such a graceful way. Found only in Madagascar, this long-legged leaper is a type of lemur called a sikafa. Agile and strong, sikafas get around on the ground by making a series of nimble, hind-legged hops. But they spend most of their time in treetops, where they sometimes get around by making spectacular leaps of more than twenty feet (six meters). Unlike other primates, sikafas leap upright, landing feet first instead of hands first.

Why are these ants carrying pieces of leaves?

Like all good gardeners, these leafcutter ants use compost, which is decaying plant matter that becomes fertilizer or food. The ants use their sharp jaws to chop off pieces of stems, leaves, and flowers from certain types of plants. They carry these plant parts back to their underground nests where they clean them and chew them up. The leafcutters use the chewed-up plant parts as compost to grow a special type of fungus that they like to eat.

What's wrong with this snake's skin?

Nothing's wrong. This black rat snake is *molting*, or shedding its skin. Depending on their age and size, snakes shed their skin several times a year. Before a snake sheds its skin, a new layer of skin grows underneath the old one. The snake gives off a fluid between the old and new layers, helping them to separate. To start actually molting, a snake will often rub its nose against a rough surface, such as a tree or rock. This helps the old skin break away from the new one underneath. After that, the snake crawls headfirst out of its old skin in a matter of minutes.

Why are these animals climbing on a car?

For the road salt that's still stuck on the car's finish. North America's bighorn sheep, like most mammals, need a precise balance of body chemicals, including body salts. These salts are important to good health. Without them, body cells cannot work properly. When some mammals can't get the body salts they need, they will travel long distances to find what are called salt licks (natural salt deposits in the wild). And when they can't find a salt lick, the road salt encrusted on the outside of an empty automobile will do just fine.

Why are all these snakes piled on top of each other?

Snakes alive! It must be spring. These red-sided garter snakes are just waking up after spending the winter clustered on top of each other in underground dens. As many as *10,000* of these snakes sometimes hibernate (enter an inactive, sleeplike state) together, twisting their tails, heads, and bodies together so that they can snuggle up to stay warm. But as soon as the weather gets warmer, they wiggle their way up and out of their dens to start searching for food. And in the case of these red-sided garters, food usually means frogs.

Odd Couples

Is this fish trapped in an underwater plant?

This may *look* like a plant, but it's actually an underwater animal called a sea anemone. These long, tubelike "leaves" are, in fact, tentacles with stinging cells that project poisonous threads. For almost any other fish, swimming into the sea anemone's open arms can be a deadly mistake. But the anemone fish, also called the clownfish, that you see here can cozy up to anemones without fear. Some scientists think that a special mucus (slippery coating) on the skin of the clownfish may prevent the anemone's stinging cells from giving off their poison. By seeking shelter within the sea anemone's tentacles, the clownfish gains protection from its enemies. It is also able to pick up leftover food from the anemone.

Why doesn't this hippo shake off these annoying little birds?

As far as this hippopotamus is concerned, these African birds, called oxpeckers or tickbirds, aren't annoying at all. In fact, they do an important job keeping the hippo *free* of annoying insects. While clinging to large animals such as hippopotamuses and elephants, oxpeckers use their wide bills and sharp claws to pick ticks and maggots from the hide. They also make a hissing sound when they are alarmed. This sound warns the hippos that danger may be near.

Why doesn't this eel gulp down the small fish?

The eel is happy to let the small fry do its job—give the eel a good cleaning. The small fish is a wrasse. Some wrasses, such as young blueheads, act as cleaners for larger fish. They pick off and eat the tiny creatures and dead pieces of skin that cling to groupers, eels, snappers, and other fish that take themselves to the "cleaners" from time to time. One type of Indo-Pacific cleaner wrasse stakes out its own turf on coral reefs, where as many as 300 fish may seek out its services in a 6-hour period. The cleaner wrasse's color and dancelike swimming motion act as a kind of undersea advertising for customers. Even large hunter fish such as this eel allow the tiny cleaners to enter and exit their throats unharmed.

Why is the smaller bird poking its head into the bigger bird's mouth?

The smaller bird, an adult white wagtail, is actually feeding the bigger bird, a baby cuckoo. The adult wagtail thinks the baby cuckoo is its *own* baby. That's because the egg containing the baby cuckoo was laid by its mother in the wagtail's nest when the wagtail was away. Some species of cuckoos (like the mother of this one) lay their eggs in the nests of other birds, such as wagtails, one egg per nest. An adult female cuckoo usually removes eggs that are already in the nest to make room for her own. Then the adult female cuckoo goes on her way, leaving the other birds to hatch and feed her chicks. Cuckoo eggs hatch before the eggs of the host bird or very shortly afterward. Then the young cuckoos try to push the host's eggs or babies out of the nest! If they don't succeed in getting rid of their nest mates, the cuckoos will beg for food so strongly that they are usually fed first and more often.

Is this bird hitching a ride?

Yes, but that's not all. This cattle egret is waiting for the cow to stir up a meal. Found in Europe, Africa, Asia, Australia, and North and South America, cattle egrets are insect eaters. They follow herds of large animals—elephants, cattle, buffalo, antelope, and horses—that graze in tall grass. The cattle egret snaps up the insects and grubs that the large animals disturb while they walk and feed. Sometimes the bird picks ticks from the animals' hides. So where the cow can't scratch a pest, the egret can snatch and snack on it. This is one hitchhiker who's always welcome by the cow.

Can you spot the fish in this picture?

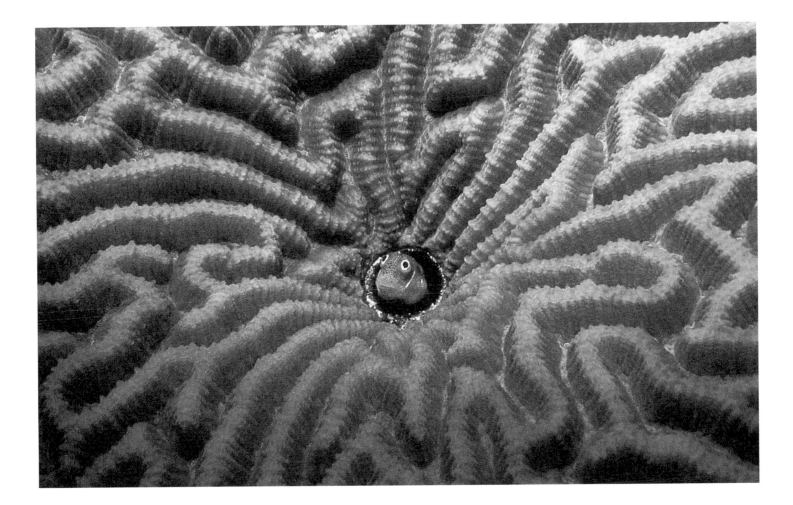

If you have trouble seeing the blenny swimming near this brain coral, then so do the blenny's enemies. The blenny is a type of small, usually ocean-dwelling fish that can be found in both warm and cold seas. Coral reefs are one of the places where it lives. Many blenny species can change color rapidly. They may pass through up to six different color phases for camouflage (coloring of an animal or species that protects it in its surroundings) or, when they are trying to attract a mate, to threaten other blennies. When a blenny changes its spots, it is hard for predators to make out its form against a background like brain coral. The fish can use its color and the coral to hide in plain sight.

Are these ants eating the white bugs?

No. The white-covered, oval-shaped insects you see here are mealybugs. They feed on citrus and other plants by sucking the juices out of leaves and stems. The waste that mealybugs give off is in the form of honeydew, a liquid that has sugar and protein in it. Some kinds of ants, like these West African black dairying ants, like to eat this honeydew. That's why the ants help, not harm, the mealybugs— they're an important producer of food for the ants. Often the ants will move the mealybugs to the most nutritious parts of plants so that they can produce even more honeydew. The ants will also fiercely defend this colony of tiny (about one-eighth inch, or three millimeters, in length), wingless, soft-bodied, slow-moving mealybugs from enemies such as birds, reptiles, and other insects. Clearly, the mealybugs and ants help each other.

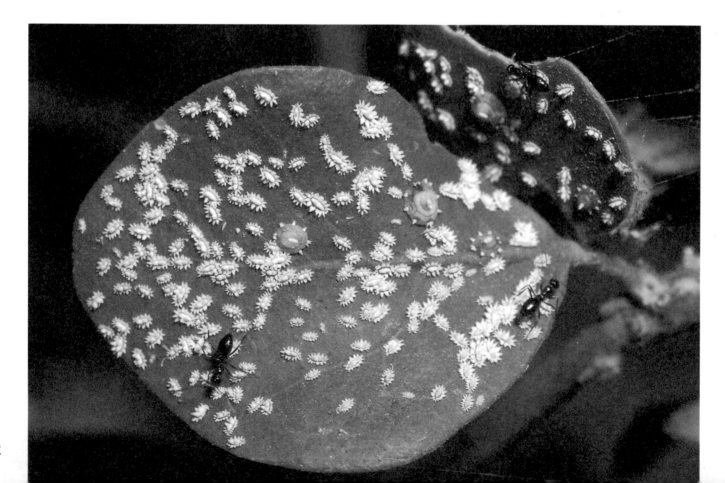

Animal
Architects

Is this animal stocking its nest with food?

Yes, the bank, or red-backed, vole likes to stock up on juicy berries and other food in its underground nest. This European animal is a burrower, and it builds a network of shallow nests under logs or tree roots in woodlands or shrubbed areas. These round nests are made out of moss, crushed wood, or fallen leaves. Usually, they are built close to the surface of the earth, but they can be up to eighteen inches (forty-six centimeters) below ground. During the day, the bank vole leaves the nest to find food. Besides berries, it eats seeds, roots, grasses, and other fruits.

What kinds of nests are these?

These nests were made from grass and twigs collected by weaverbirds. The name of these birds comes from what they do best—weave (lace together) nests. The long, pouchlike nests are round or oval, and they hang down from the branches of tall trees. The black-headed weaver of Africa (see large photo) nests in colonies, which are large groups of birds that live together and build their homes near each other. The shy redheaded weaver, also of Africa, lives in small groups, and the male (see photo top right) builds a nest for each of his mates. In Asia, the baya weaver lives in colonies and builds nests with long entrance tubes at the bottom (see photo bottom right).

Do fish build nests?

Some do, like the three-spined stickleback species of Europe and North America that you see here. These two photos are both of the same male stickleback. On the right, he's carrying an underwater twig to the nest he's building around a hole he had dug with his fins. Once the nest of plant parts is built, he seals it all together with a sticky liquid from his kidneys. Afterward, he swims through the nest to make an opening and then does a dance to attract a female into it. Once the female is inside, she lays her eggs. When the female leaves the nest after laying her eggs, the male slips back in and fertilizes them (see lefthand photo). Several days later, the eggs hatch. The father watches over the young fish until they can fend for themselves. He even carries them back to the nest in his mouth if there is danger. It is the male stickleback, not the female, who basically raises the babies.

How did these hornets build their nest?

Bit by bit. Large members of the wasp family, hornets gnaw off pieces of wood or bark and mix them with their saliva (liquid formed in the mouth) to make a kind of fragile paper. They use this paper for their nests, which are often made under the roofs of buildings. In the spring, a mated female hornet, called the queen, makes several tiny, six-sided, paper cells in which she lays her eggs. When the baby hornets of this first brood hatch and grow up, they help enlarge the nest. As more and more of the cells are made, they become clusters that are called combs. These combs are covered by the hornets with a paper shell like the one you see here. Sometimes hornet nests get as big as basketballs, and some nests hold hundreds of hornets.

How do beavers build dams?

At night, along the banks of rivers and lakes, pairs of North American beavers build dams and lodges using only their paws and long, ever-growing teeth (see photo top right). The dams are made of logs and branches cut down or found by the beavers, who pack them together with clay and dead leaves. The lodges are made with the same materials (see large photo). Near the lodges, beavers keep piles of leaves, twigs, branches, and tree bark as an underwater food supply during the winter months. The only entrances into the lodge are from below water (see photo bottom right of beaver entering lodge), and beavers need only swim into the water below their lodges to find their stored food. Beavers usually swim underwater for just a few minutes at a time, but sometimes they can stay underwater for up to twenty minutes!

What are hummingbird nests made of?

Female hummingbirds build delicate little cup-shaped nests with thick walls of moss or bark and lined with feathers, hair, flower stems, and other soft material to keep the eggs and small birds warm. These North and Central American birds use

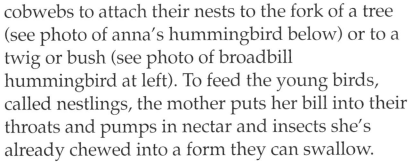

cobwebs to attach their nests to the fork of a tree (see photo of anna's hummingbird below) or to a twig or bush (see photo of broadbill hummingbird at left). To feed the young birds, called nestlings, the mother puts her bill into their throats and pumps in nectar and insects she's already chewed into a form they can swallow.

Is this bee stuck in a hole?

Not at all. When the aptly named carpenter bee is ready to lay her eggs, she selects a hollow twig, dried stem, or a post of dry wood and chews out a nest hole. She uses strong, sharp jaws called *mandibles* to bore her way into the wood. Once the hole has been dug, the female carpenter bee puts a lot of pollen (a yellowish powder) from the flowers of nearby plants into it. Then she lays an egg in the hole and covers it with bits of wood held together by saliva. The female makes ten to fifteen similar holes, called brood cells, in a row. Carpenter bees thrive in Africa and other warm regions, and they also live in the more mild climate of Central Europe. They stay in groups during the winter and mate in the spring.

Is this mouse playing hide-and-seek?

It's probably playing more "hide" than "seek" if an enemy (cat, dog, owl, fox, hawk, snake, coyote, or rat) is approaching. But in this case, the harvest mouse is simply coming out of its nest. Because they are so tiny (a full-grown one weighs only a quarter ounce, or seven grams), these North American mice build nests that are not much bigger than tennis balls. The nests are made of thin strips of grass and have one or two entrances near the bottom. They are built in tall grasses or shrubs near supplies of food—mostly seeds, plants, and insects. In the winter, harvest mice will sometimes build their nests in the underground tunnels of other rodents. Litters of up to a dozen harvest mice are born inside these nests.

Why was this nest made of dirt?

The birds that made this nest are rufous horneros, and their well-designed, tightly packed dirt nests provide strong protection against sun, wind, and flying predators from above. The nest was actually made of straw and plenty of mud, which then dried and hardened. *Hornero* is Spanish for "baker," and these rufous horneros (or rufous ovenbirds) build nests that are shaped like bakers' ovens—round with a domed top. The mud and straw nest is often built on the top of a fence post, a house, or (as in this photo) in the fork of a tree. Usually, the nest has a narrow entrance hole as well as a passageway that leads to an eight-inch-wide (twenty-centimeter-wide) nesting area lined with soft grass. Though it takes months to build such strong nests, these South American birds make new ones every year. Other birds make use of the rufous horneros' old nests.

Index

Page numbers for definitions are in italics